COUNTRY
TEATIME
RECIPES

*Traditional treats
for the tea table*

*with illustrations by
Terry Whitworth*

SALMON

Index

Bath Buns   14
Bristol Cake   39
Cornish Figgie Hobbin   8
Cornish Ginger Fairings   47
Cornish Heavy Cake   43
Cornish Luncheon Cake   38
Cornish Pitchy Cake   18
Cornish Rich Plum Cake   32
Cornish Saffron Cake   6
Cornish Store Cake   30
Cornish Sultana Cake   23
Cornish Yeast Cake   15
Devon Flats   31
Devonshire Apple Gingerbread   45
Devonshire Apple Scones   11
Devonshire Biscuits   42
Devonshire Cider Cake   35

Devonshire Potato Cake   26
Devonshire Revel Buns   19
Devonshire Scones   5
Devonshire Splits   7
Dorset Apple Cake   29
Dorset Digestive Biscuits   40
Dorset Potato Scones   34
Dorset Rock Cakes   22
Dorset Teabread   13
Penzance Cake   27
Somerset Apple Sauce Cake   16
Somerset Cheese & Apple Loaf   37
Somerset Easter Cakes   10
Somerset Teabread   46
West Country Dripping Cake   3
Widecombe Fair Gingerbread   24
Wiltshire Buttermilk Cake   21

Cover pictures *front:* Cottages at Selworthy *back:* Newton Ferrers by Donald Greig
title page: Church Steps, Minehead

Printed and Published by J. Salmon Ltd., Sevenoaks, England © Copyright

West Country Dripping Cake

A light, smooth-tasting family fruit cake which uses dripping instead of the more usual butter as the fat content.

8 oz flour	2 oz currants
1/2 teaspoon bicarbonate of soda	2 oz sultanas
1/2 teaspoon grated nutmeg	1 oz chopped mixed peel
4 oz dripping	2 eggs, beaten
4 oz soft brown sugar	Milk to mix

Set oven to 350° F or Mark 4. Grease and line a 6 to 7 inch cake tin. Sift the flour, bicarbonate of soda and nutmeg into a bowl and rub in the dripping until the mixture resembles breadcrumbs. Add the sugar, dried fruit and mixed peel and mix in the beaten eggs and just sufficient milk to produce a dropping consistency. Put into the tin, make a slight hollow in the centre and bake for about 1 to 1 1/4 hours or until a skewer inserted comes out clean. Leave to cool in the tin and turn out on to a wire rack.

Cottages at Manaton

Devonshire Scones

Rich, buttery scones served split and filled with lots of homemade jam and Clotted Cream.

1 lb self-raising flour	**4 oz sugar**
1 teaspoon salt	**2 eggs**
6 oz butter, softened	**5 fl.oz milk**

Beaten egg for glazing

Set oven to 450° F or Mark 8. Grease baking sheets. Sift the flour and salt into a bowl and rub in the butter until the mixture resembles breadcrumbs. Stir in the sugar and make a well in the centre. Drop in the eggs and gradually add the milk, working in the flour from the sides until the dough is smooth and elastic. Transfer to a floured surface and roll out lightly to a full ½ inch thick. Cut out rounds with a 2½ inch cutter, brush with beaten egg and place on the baking sheet. Bake for about 8 to 10 minutes until golden. Transfer to a wire rack to cool. Makes about 18 scones.

Cornish Saffron Cake

This old English cake or sweet bread which originated in Cornwall is made from saffron flavoured yeast dough with currants and candied peel.

1 teaspoon saffron, dried in the oven and rolled to a powder
1 oz yeast   1 pint tepid water   Pinch of sugar   2 lb flour   Pinch of salt
1 lb butter, softened   8 oz sugar   1 lb currants   2 oz chopped mixed peel

Soak the saffron overnight in 3 tablespoons of boiling water. Set oven to 375°F or Mark 5. Grease two 1 lb loaf tins. Mix the yeast in the 1 pint of tepid water with a pinch of sugar and a cup of the flour and leave in a warm place until frothy. Sieve the remaining flour and the salt into a bowl and rub in the butter under the mixture resembles breadcrumbs. Mix in the sugar then add the dried fruit and peel. Pour the yeast mixture into the dry ingredients and add the saffron water. Mix to a soft dough, adding more tepid water if necessary and knead well; return to the lightly oiled or floured bowl, cover and put in a warm place to rise until doubled in size. Then knead the dough again until any air bubbles have gone. Divide and put into the tins. Allow to prove for 20 to 30 minutes in a warm place. Bake for 1 hour or until a skewer inserted comes out clean. Turn out on to a wire rack to cool. This mixture can also be shaped into little buns and baked for ½ hour at 400°F or Mark 6.

Devonshire Splits

This sweet dough bun is split and filled with home made jam and cream for the traditional Clotted Cream Tea. Cornish Splits are similar.

½ oz fresh yeast	1 lb strong white flour
1 teaspoon caster sugar	1 teaspoon salt
½ pint tepid milk	2 oz butter, softened
1 oz caster sugar	

Flour baking sheets. Mix together the yeast, teaspoon of caster sugar and milk and leave in a warm place until frothy. Sieve the flour and salt into a bowl, rub in the butter until the mixture resembles breadcrumbs and stir in the sugar. Add the yeast liquid and mix to a soft dough. Knead on a floured surface until elastic, return to the lightly oiled or floured bowl, cover and leave in a warm place to rise until doubled in size. Knock back, knead again, divide into 16 pieces, mould into bun shapes and place on the baking sheet. Cover and leave in the warm until well risen. Meanwhile set oven to 425ºF or Mark 7. When risen, bake for about 15 minutes until pale golden. Cool on a wire rack.

Cornish Figgie Hobbin

A dried fig slice made with suet and lard.

8 oz flour	**2 oz lard**
3/4 teaspoon baking powder	**8 oz dried figs, chopped**
2 oz chopped suet	**2-3 fl.oz milk**

Set oven to 400° F or Mark 6. Grease baking sheets. Sift the flour and baking powder into a bowl, rub in the suet and lard and mix in the chopped figs. Blend in sufficient milk to produce a stiff dough. Roll out on a floured surface to 1/2 inch thickness and cut into 4 inch squares. Put on the baking sheet, score the surfaces lightly with a knife and bake for about 30 minutes until golden. Transfer to a wire rack to cool.

The Old Post Office, Tintagel

Somerset Easter Cakes

Spicy, fruit cookies mixed with brandy.

8 oz flour	**$^1/_2$ teaspoon ground cinnamon**
4 oz butter, softened	**$^1/_2$ teaspoon mixed spice**
4 oz caster sugar	**1 egg, beaten**
4 oz currants	**2 tablespoons brandy**

Set oven to 350° F or Mark 4. Grease baking sheets. Sift the flour into a bowl and rub in the butter until mixture resembles breadcrumbs. Stir in the sugar, currants and spices. Beat together the egg and brandy and blend into the mixture to produce a stiff consistency. Knead the mixture on a floured surface and roll out to $^1/_2$ inch thickness. Cut into rounds with a $2^1/_2$ inch cutter and put on the baking sheet. Bake for about 20 minutes until golden. Transfer to a wire rack to cool.

Devonshire Apple Scones

Unlike normal scones, these scones resemble rock buns and have a pleasant apple flavour.
Serve split and buttered as usual.

8 oz wholemeal self-raising flour
1 teaspoon ground cinnamon
1 teaspoon baking powder
4 oz butter, softened

2 oz soft brown sugar
2 medium size cooking apples,
**   peeled, cored and finely diced**
1 medium egg, beaten

Set oven to 375ºF or Mark 5. Flour baking sheets. Sieve the flour, cinnamon and baking powder together into a bowl and rub in the butter until the mixture resembles breadcrumbs. Stir in the sugar and apple and lastly stir in the egg. Form the mixture into 10 or 12 rough heaps (as for rock buns) on the baking sheet and bake for 20 to 25 minutes until lightly browned. Allow to cool slightly before transferring to a wire rack. Serve with butter.

Gold Hill, Shaftesbury

Dorset Teabread

Dried fruit boiled in tea and mixed with wheatmeal flour and spices produce this succulent teabread.

1 cup of tea (no milk)   6 oz butter   8 oz soft brown sugar
12 oz mixed dried fruit (can include some chopped walnuts, if liked)
12 oz self-raising wheatmeal flour   1 teaspoon ground mixed spice
1 teaspoon ground cinnamon   3 medium eggs, beaten

Set oven to 325°F or Mark 3. Grease and line an 8 inch cake tin. Put the tea, butter, sugar and dried fruit into a large saucepan and simmer gently for 15 minutes until the fruit is plump. Remove from the heat, allow to cool and then beat in the flour, spices and eggs. Put into the tin and bake for about 2 hours or until a skewer inserted comes out clean. Turn out on to a wire rack to cool and serve sliced, plain or buttered.

Bath Buns

These well known yeast buns were originally made in the city of Bath around 1700.
The coarse sugar topping is their distinguishing feature.

1 lb strong white flour $\frac{1}{2}$ teaspoon salt   2 oz butter, softened
2 oz caster sugar   4 oz sultanas   2 oz chopped mixed peel
1 oz fresh yeast $\frac{1}{2}$ pint tepid milk   2 medium eggs, beaten
TOPPING
Beaten egg   Coarse sugar crystals

Grease baking sheets. Sieve the flour and salt into a bowl and rub in the butter until the mixture resembles breadcrumbs. Stir in the sugar, sultanas and mixed peel. Blend the yeast with a little of the tepid milk to a smooth cream. Make a well in the centre of the flour, add the yeast liquid, the beaten eggs and remaining milk and mix to a soft dough. Knead on a lightly floured surface until smooth. Return to the lightly oiled or floured bowl, cover with a cloth and leave to rise in a warm place until doubled in size. Re-knead the dough and divide into 16 even size pieces. Shape into rounds and place, well spaced, on the baking sheet. Cover and leave to prove in a warm place until doubled in size. Meanwhile set oven to 375°F or Mark 5. Brush with egg, sprinkle with coarse sugar crystals and bake for 20 minutes until golden. Cool on a wire rack and serve buttered.

Cornish Yeast Cake

This mixture can be used either to make a currant dough cake or individual currant buns.

1 oz yeast	Pinch of salt
2 oz sugar	2 oz butter, softened
½ pint tepid milk	2 oz lard
1 lb flour	4 oz currants and/or sultanas
2 oz chopped mixed peel	

Set oven to 400°F or Mark 6. Grease a 7 inch cake tin or a baking sheet if making buns. Mix together the yeast and a teaspoon of the sugar, add the milk and set aside in a warm place to sponge. Sift the flour and salt into a bowl and rub in the fats until the mixture resembles breadcrumbs. Stir in the remaining sugar, the dried fruit and peel, then work in the yeast mixture and knead well. Return to the lightly greased or floured bowl and leave to rise in a warm place until doubled in size. Knock back, knead again and put into the tin or make into buns. Allow to prove in the warm for about 20 minutes. When risen, bake the cake for about 30 minutes or until a skewer inserted comes out clean or the buns for about 15 to 20 minutes. Leave to cool and turn out on to a wire rack.

Somerset Apple Sauce Cake

A well spiced, moist cake covered with butter icing.

4 oz butter
8 oz soft brown sugar
1 egg, beaten
6 oz apple sauce, unsweetened
8 oz self-raising flour

$^1/_2$ **teaspoon ground cinnamon**
$^1/_2$ **teaspoon ground cloves**
$^1/_2$ **teaspoon ground nutmeg**
$^1/_2$ **teaspoon salt**
4 oz raisins

Vanilla flavoured butter icing

If necessary, first make the apple sauce by boiling to a pulp sufficient peeled and chopped cooking apples, preferably Bramley, with a very little water. Allow to cool. Set oven to 350° F or Mark 4. Grease and line an 8 inch cake tin. Cream the butter and sugar together in a bowl until light and fluffy. Gradually beat in the egg and then stir in the apple sauce. Sift in the flour, spices and salt, add the raisins and mix well together. Put into the tin and bake for about 1 hour or until a skewer inserted comes out clean. Leave to cool for a few minutes in the tin and turn out on to a wire rack. When cold cover with vanilla flavoured butter icing. For the butter icing, blend together 4 oz soft margarine, 8 oz sieved icing sugar and a few drops of vanilla essence.

Lorna Doone Farm, Malmsmead

Cornish Pitchy Cake

A dough cake which gets its name from the lard, dried fruit and sugar being 'pitched' into the prepared dough.

$^1/_2$ oz fresh yeast	$^3/_4$ pint tepid water
$^1/_2$ tablespoon sugar	8 oz lard, cut into small pieces
$1^1/_2$ lbs strong white flour	4 oz currants
$^1/_2$ tablespoon salt	4 oz sugar

Grease a 2 lb loaf tin. First cream the yeast with the $^1/_2$ tablespoon of sugar. Sift the flour and salt into a bowl and mix to a smooth dough with the creamed yeast, adding the water gradually until the dough leaves the sides of the bowl cleanly. Knead well on a floured surface, return to the lightly greased or floured bowl, cover with a clean cloth and leave in a warm place to rise until doubled in size. Meanwhile, set oven to 425°F or Mark 7. When risen, knock back the dough and work in the lard, cut into small pieces, with the currants and the sugar. Knead again, put into the tin and leave to prove in the warm. Bake for about $1^1/_2$ hours until browned on top and the bottom of the loaf sounds hollow when tapped. Turn out on a wire rack to cool.

Devonshire Revel Buns

Spicy yeast buns mixed with cream which were traditionally made for village festivals.

2 - 3 tablespoons saffron milk	$\frac{1}{2}$ tablespoon sugar
1 lb flour	2 oz lard
2 teaspoons salt	5 fl. oz Devon cream
Pinch ground cinnamon	1 egg, beaten
$\frac{1}{2}$ oz fresh yeast	6 oz currants

Icing sugar for dusting

For the saffron milk, dissolve a pinch of saffron in the milk and leave to stand, preferably overnight. Sift the flour, salt and cinnamon into a bowl. Cream the yeast with the sugar. Melt the lard in a pan over a low heat with the saffron milk. Combine the yeast and the milk/lard mixture with the flour in the bowl, add the cream and the beaten egg and mix to a smooth dough. Knead thoroughly on a floured surface, return to the lightly oiled or floured bowl, cover and leave in a warm place to rise until doubled in size. Meanwhile set oven to 375°F or Mark 5. Grease baking sheets. When risen, knock back the dough and work in the currants. Shape into small buns with floured hands, put on the baking sheet and leave in the warm to prove. Bake for about 35 to 45 minutes until golden and transfer to a wire rack to cool. When cool, sprinkle the buns with icing sugar.

The Village, Castle Combe

Wiltshire Buttermilk Cake

This farmhouse fruit cake is richly spiced. Other versions appear in various forms all over the country.

1 lb flour	**4 oz brown sugar**
1 teaspoon bicarbonate of soda	**4 oz raisins**
$^1/_2$ teaspoon mixed spice	**4 oz sultanas**
$^1/_2$ teaspoon ground ginger	**4 oz currants**
$^1/_4$ teaspoon ground cinnamon	**Grated rind of half a lemon**
6 oz butter, softened	**$^1/_4$ pint buttermilk**

Set oven to 325° F or Mark 3. Grease and base line an 8 inch cake tin. Sift together into a bowl the flour, bicarbonate of soda and spices, then rub in the butter until the mixture resembles breadcrumbs. Stir in the sugar, dried fruit and lemon rind. Warm the buttermilk slightly, then stir into the mixture to form a soft dough, adding a little extra buttermilk if it is too stiff. Put into the tin and smooth over the top. Bake for 1 hour then reduce oven to 300°F or Mark 2 and bake for a further 40 to 45 minutes or until a skewer inserted comes out clean, covering the top with a piece of baking paper if it appears to be browning too quickly. Cool in the tin then turn out on to a wire rack.

Dorset Rock Cakes

These fruity rock buns are best eaten fresh on the day they are made but they also freeze well so can be stored for future use.

8 oz self-raising wheatmeal flour   **$\frac{1}{2}$ teaspoon ground mixed spice**
$\frac{1}{2}$ teaspoon ground cinnamon   **4 oz butter, softened**   **4 oz Demerara sugar**
4 oz mixed dried fruit (currants, sultanas, mixed peel, glacé cherries, etc. in any proportion)
Grated rind of half a lemon   **1 medium egg**   **2 tablespoons milk**

Set oven to 375° F or Mark 5. Grease baking sheets. Sift the flour, mixed spice and cinnamon into a bowl and rub in the butter until the mixture resembles breadcrumbs. Stir in the sugar, dried fruit and lemon rind. Add the egg and milk and combine with the dry ingredients to form a crumbly dough. Form into 10 or 12 rough heats on the baking sheet. Bake for approximately 20 minutes until lightly browned. Cool on the baking sheet for 5 minutes before transferring to a wire rack.

Cornish Sultana Cake

A plain fruit loaf.

1¹/₂ lbs flour	**1 teaspoon caster sugar**
1 dessertspoon salt	**³/₄ pint tepid water**
6 oz lard or butter	**4 oz sultanas**
¹/₂ oz fresh yeast	**Chopped lemon peel (optional)**

Grease a 2 lb loaf tin. Sift the flour and salt into a bowl and rub in the fat until the mixture resembles breadcrumbs. Cream the yeast with the sugar and a little tepid water and add to the flour. Blend in sufficient of the remaining tepid water to mix to a soft dough that leaves the side of the bowl clean. Knead thoroughly on a floured surface, return to the lightly oiled or floured bowl, cover and leave to rise in a warm place until doubled in size. Meanwhile set oven to 400ºF or Mark 6. When risen, knock back and work in the currants and the lemon peel (if used). Put into the tin and leave in the warm to prove. Bake for about 1 to 1¹/₂ hours until brown on top and the bottom of the loaf sounds hollow when tapped. Transfer to a wire rack to cool. Serve sliced and buttered.

Widecombe Fair Gingerbreads

Simple ginger fairing biscuits.

6 oz flour   1 teaspoon ground ginger   5 oz butter, softened
6 oz caster sugar   6 oz black treacle

Set oven to 350° F or Mark 4. Grease baking sheets. Sift the flour and ginger into a bowl and rub in the butter until the mixture resembles breadcrumbs. Stir in the sugar. Melt the treacle in a pan over a low heat and blend in to the flour mixture to produce a soft consistency. Drop spoonsful of the mixture well apart on to the baking sheet. Bake for about 30 to 40 minutes until firm yet springy to the touch. Leave to cool for a few minutes and transfer to a wire rack.

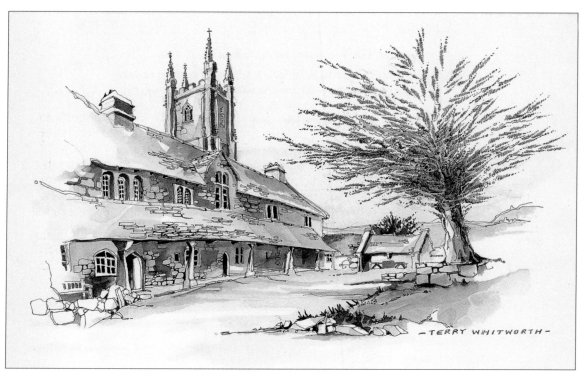

Widecome-in-the-Moor

Devonshire Potato Cake

An unusual, spicy teabread made with mashed potato.

6 oz flour   **¹/₂ teaspoon mixed spice**   **1 teaspoon baking powder**
2 oz butter, softened   **6 oz cooked cold mashed potatoes**
4 oz brown sugar   **8 oz currants**
¹/₂ oz caraway seeds   **2 eggs, beaten**

Set oven to 400° F or Mark 6. Well grease a shallow cake tin. If necessary, first boil and mash sufficient potatoes and leave to cool. Sift the flour, spice and baking powder into a bowl and rub in the butter until the mixture resembles breadcrumbs. Stir in the mashed potato, sugar, currants and caraway seeds, add the beaten eggs and mix well together. Put into the tin and smooth out. Bake for about 30 minutes until golden. Turn out, cut into squares and serve warm.

Penzance Cake

A very fruity cake made with a plain mixture.

1 lb flour	**1 lb currants**
$^1/_2$ teaspoon bicarbonate of soda	**8 oz chopped crystallised ginger**
4 oz butter, softened	**4 oz chopped mixed peel**
2 teaspoons ground cinnamon	**2 eggs, beaten**
	5 fl.oz tepid milk

Set oven to 350º F or Mark 4. Grease and line a 9 to 10 inch cake tin. Sift the flour and bicarbonate of soda into a bowl and rub in the butter until the mixture resembles breadcrumbs. Add the cinnamon, currants, ginger and mixed peel and mix to a soft consistency with the beaten eggs and milk. Put into the tin and bake for about 2 hours or until a skewer inserted comes out clean. Leave to cool in the tin and turn out on to a wire rack.

Thomas Hardy's Birthplace, Bockhampton

Dorset Apple Cake

A moist cake or pudding made with apple, currants and peel with a crunchy topping.
Devon Apple Cake is similar but omits the fruit and is topped with granulated sugar.

8 oz self-raising flour   1 teaspoon salt   4 oz butter, softened
4 oz caster sugar   1 lb cooking apples, peeled, cored and diced
1 medium egg, beaten   2 oz currants
1 oz chopped mixed peel   1 oz Demerara sugar for sprinkling

Set oven to 375° F or Mark 5. Well grease an 8 inch round cake tin. Sift the flour and salt into a bowl and rub in the butter until the mixture resembles breadcrumbs. Stir in the sugar, diced apple and egg and mix well. Add the currants and peel and stir in. Put into the tin, sprinkle the top with Demerara sugar and bake for 30 to 40 minutes until golden and a skewer inserted comes out clean. Cool in the tin and turn out on to a wire rack. Serve, sliced spread with butter or, alternatively, serve warm with Clotted Cream as a pudding.

Cornish Store Cake

A fruit cake which is useful to have as a stand-by in the cupboard to use as required.

8 oz margarine	6 oz sultanas
8 oz caster sugar	3 oz glacé cherries, quartered
4 eggs, beaten	3 oz chopped mixed peel
12 oz flour	2 oz blanched almonds, chopped
6 oz currants	Grated rind of 1 lemon

Set oven to 350°F or Mark 4. Grease and line an 8 inch cake tin. In a bowl, cream together the margarine and sugar until light and fluffy. Beat in the eggs gradually, fold in the flour and add the dried fruit, glacé cherries, peel, almonds and lemon rind. Put into the tin and bake for 2½ hours or until a skewer inserted comes out clean. Leave to cool in the tin and turn out on to a wire rack.

Devon Flats

Delicious crunchy biscuits with a creamy taste.

1 lb flour	**8 oz caster sugar**
$\frac{1}{2}$ pint Devon cream	**1 egg, beaten**
Milk to mix	

Set oven to 425° F or Mark 7. Grease baking sheets. Put the cream into a bowl, sift in the flour and mix together. Add the sugar and beaten egg and mix with just sufficient milk to give a smooth, stiff dough. Roll out very thinly on a lightly floured surface and cut into rounds with a 2 inch cutter. Put on the baking sheet and bake for about 10 minutes until golden. Transfer to a wire rack to cool.

Cornish Rich Plum Cake

An extremely fruity cake which is suitable for a special occasion.

8 oz butter	4 oz glacé cherries, halved
8 oz caster sugar	8 oz flour
6 medium eggs, lightly beaten	8 oz chopped mixed peel
8 oz currants	8 oz almonds, blanched and chopped
8 oz raisins	2 tablespoons rum or brandy
8 oz sultanas	1 tablespoon black coffee

Set oven to 325°F or Mark 3. Grease a 9 inch round cake tin. In a bowl, cream together the butter and sugar until light and fluffy. Stir in the lightly beaten eggs one at a time with a teaspoon of flour after the third egg. Beat thoroughly. Mix all the dried fruit together with half the flour. Stir the rest of the flour, together with the peel and almonds, into the egg and butter mixture. Then add the floured fruit, the rum or brandy and the coffee. Put in the tin and bake for 2½ hours or longer until a skewer inserted comes out clean. To prevent the sides from burning, tie a band of brown paper round the outside of the tin before baking. Leave to cool in the tin and turn out on to a wire rack.

Towards the Harbour, St. Mawes

Dorset Potato Scones

These plain scones are quick and easy to make and are excellent eaten just buttered
or with cheese or jam. They stay fresh longer than ordinary scones.

9 oz self-raising flour   **3 oz butter, softened**
$\frac{1}{2}$ teaspoon salt   **6 oz cooked cold mashed potatoes**
3 tablespoons ($2\frac{1}{2}$ fl.oz) milk

If necessary, first boil and mash sufficient potatoes and leave to cool. Set oven to
425°F or Mark 7. Flour baking sheets. Sieve the flour and salt together into a bowl
and rub in the butter until the mixture resembles breadcrumbs. Mix in the mashed
potatoes and stir in the milk a little at a time, sufficient to make a soft dough. Roll
out on a floured surface to about $\frac{1}{2}$ inch thickness and cut into about 12 to 15 even-
size triangles. Transfer to the baking sheet and bake for about 15 minutes until
golden. Transfer to a wire rack to cool. Serve split and well buttered, either warm
or cold.

Devonshire Cider Cake

A plain cake flavoured with cinnamon and mixed with cider to give it a distinctive flavour.

4 oz butter	**1 teaspoon cinnamon**
4 oz caster sugar	**8 oz self-raising flour**
2 medium eggs, beaten	**¹/₂ pint cider**

Set oven to 350°F or Mark 4. Grease and line a 7 inch round cake tin. In a bowl, cream the butter and sugar together until light and fluffy. Stir in the eggs, cinnamon and half of the flour. Gradually add the cider to this mixture and lastly add the remaining flour and mix thoroughly. Put into the tin and bake for about 45 minutes until firm to the touch, golden in colour and a skewer inserted comes out clean. Leave to cool and turn out on to a wire rack.

The Yarn Market, Dunster

Somerset Cheese and Apple Loaf

A moist apple teabread with grated cheese and chopped nuts.

4 oz butter, softened   6 oz caster sugar   2 eggs, beaten
8 oz unpeeled grated apple (including juice)   4 oz Cheddar cheese, grated
2 oz chopped mixed nuts   1 lb flour $\frac{1}{2}$ oz baking powder
$\frac{1}{2}$ teaspoon bicarbonate of soda $\frac{1}{2}$ tablespoon salt

Set oven to 350° F or Mark 4. Grease a 2 lb loaf tin. Cream the butter and sugar together in a bowl until light and fluffy and add the eggs, apple, cheese and the nuts. Sift together the flour, baking powder, bicarbonate of soda and salt, combine with the butter etc. mixture and mix well. Put the mixture into the tin and bake for about $1\frac{1}{2}$ to 2 hours until brown on top and the bottom of the loaf sounds hollow when tapped. Turn out on a wire rack to cool. Serve sliced and buttered.

Cornish Luncheon Cake

A light sherry-flavoured fruit cake which is nice eaten on its own or with a glass of fortified wine.

6 oz butter, softened	2 teaspoons salt
6 oz caster sugar	1 teacup warm milk and water mixed
3 eggs	8 oz sultanas
1 lb flour	2 oz chopped mixed peel
1 dessertspoon baking powder	$^1/_2$ wine glass sweet sherry

Set oven to 375° F or Mark 5. Grease an 8 inch round cake tin. In a bowl, cream together the butter and sugar until light and fluffy. Add the eggs one at a time, beating to a creamy mixture. Sieve together the flour, baking powder and salt and gradually stir into the butter mixture alternately with the milk/water, a little at a time. Just before all the flour is used up, add the sultanas and peel, then the last of the flour and the sherry. Put into the tin and bake for 1 hour then reduce oven to 350°F or Mark 4 and continue for about another hour or until a skewer inserted comes out clean. Leave to cool in the tin then turn out on to a wire rack.

Bristol Cake

A useful plain cake with plenty of sultanas; quick to make but not a keeper.

1 lb flour	**6 oz caster sugar**
1½ teaspoons baking powder	**8 oz sultanas**
6 oz butter, softened	**3 eggs, lightly beaten**

Set oven to 350° F or Mark 4. Grease and line a 6 to 7 inch cake tin. Sift the flour and baking powder into a bowl and rub in the butter until the mixture resembles breadcrumbs. Stir in the sugar and sultanas and mix with the lightly beaten eggs to a dropping consistency. Put into the tin and bake for about 1½ to 2 hours or until a skewer inserted comes out clean. Leave to cool for a few minutes in the tin and turn out on to a wire rack.

Dorset Digestive Biscuits

These wholemeal biscuits can be served plain or buttered; they go well with cheese,
particularly the distinctive Blue Vinney Cheese from their native county.

6 oz self-raising wholemeal flour	**3 oz butter, softened**
2 oz fine oatmeal	**1 oz soft brown sugar**
1 level teaspoon salt	**4 tablespoons milk**

Set oven to 375° F or Mark 5. Flour baking sheets. Put the flour, oatmeal and salt into a bowl and rub in the butter until the mixture resembles breadcrumbs. Stir in the sugar and enough milk to bind to a firm dough. Roll out on a floured surface to ¼ inch thickness. Cut into rounds with a 3 inch cutter and prick evenly all over with a fork. Transfer to the baking sheet and bake for approximately 20 minutes until lightly browned. Cool slightly before transferring to a wire rack.

Cottages at Cerne Abbas

Devonshire Biscuits

A sweet biscuit incorporating ground almonds.

8 oz flour	**1 oz ground almonds**
4 oz butter, softened	**2 egg yolks**
4 oz caster sugar	**Milk to mix**

Set oven to 350°F or Mark 4. Grease baking sheets. Sift the flour into a bowl and rub in the butter until the mixture resembles breadcrumbs. Add the sugar and ground almonds and egg yolks and mix to a stiff paste, adding a little milk if necessary. Roll out on a floured surface to $1/4$ inch thickness and cut into rounds with a $2^1/2$ inch cutter. Put the biscuits on to the baking sheet, prick with a fork and bake for about 15 minutes until golden. Transfer to a wire rack to cool.

Cornish Heavy Cake

Not really a cake but a fruit slice made with puff pastry.

1 lb flour	3 oz sultanas
Pinch of salt	3 oz currants
12 oz butter, diced	2 oz lemon peel, chopped
4 oz lard, diced	Cold water to mix

Milk for glazing

Set oven to 450° F or Mark 8. Grease a baking sheet. Sift the flour and salt into a bowl. Divide the fat into 4 equal parts. Rub one quarter into the flour until the mixture is soft and crumbly. Add the dried fruit and peel and mix with just enough cold water to give an elastic dough. Knead lightly, turn out on to a floured surface and roll out to a rectangle. Dot two thirds of the pastry with another quarter of the fat, fold the plain piece over one third, then the other third on top and roll out. Repeat the process of dotting, folding and rolling twice more to use up the fat. Finally, roll out to a rectangle ¾ to 1 inch thick, score the surface with a diamond pattern with a sharp knife and brush with milk. Put on to the baking sheet and bake for 10 minutes, then reduce oven to 400°F or Mark 6 for a further 20 minutes until golden brown. Cool and cut into squares.

The Square, Hope Cove

Devonshire Apple Gingerbread

A variation on the gingerbread theme including chopped apple flavoured with ground cloves.

**2 oz butter   2 oz caster sugar   1½ oz golden syrup
4 oz flour   ½ teaspoon bicarbonate of soda
1 teaspoon ground ginger   ½ teaspoon ground cloves
12 oz cooking apples, peeled, cored and finely chopped
Milk to mix   Cinnamon flavoured icing**

Set oven to 350° F or Mark 4. Grease and line a shallow 8 inch cake tin. Melt the butter, sugar and syrup in a large pan over a gentle heat. Remove from the heat. Sift together the flour, bicarbonate of soda and spices and blend in to the mixture in the pan. Add the chopped apple and mix with sufficient milk to produce a dropping consistency. Spoon into the tin and bake for about 1½ hours until a skewer inserted comes out clean. Turn out on to a wire rack to cool and when cold cover the top with cinnamon icing and cut into squares. Make the icing with icing sugar and water and a pinch of ground cinnamon.

Somerset Teabread

Chopped apple with raisins soaked in cider give this teatime loaf a moist texture and juicy flavour.

3 oz raisins soaked in 2 tablespoons cider
8 oz self-raising flour   ¼ teaspoon salt   1 level teaspoon mixed spice
4 oz butter, softened   3 oz soft brown sugar
1 medium cooking apple, peeled, cored and finely chopped
2 medium eggs, beaten
GLAZE
2 oz soft brown sugar   2 tablespoons cider

Set oven to 350° F or Mark 4. Grease a 2 lb loaf tin. First put the raisins to soak in 2 tablespoons of cider. Sieve the flour, salt and spice into a bowl and rub in the butter until the mixture resembles breadcrumbs. Stir in the sugar, the finely chopped apple and the raisin/cider mixture, add the eggs and mix well. Put the mixture into the tin and bake for approximately 1 hour until golden and a skewer inserted comes out clean. Turn out on to a wire rack to cool. Boil the glaze ingredients together in a pan for 3 or 4 minutes and brush over the warm loaf. Serve sliced, plain or buttered.

Cornish Ginger Fairings

These spicy ginger biscuits were traditionally sold at Cornish country fairs and today are popular with visitors to the county.

4 oz flour	1 teaspoon mixed spice
1 teaspoon baking powder	1 oz grated lemon peel
1 teaspoon bicarbonate of soda	2 oz brown sugar
1 teaspoon ground cinnamon	2 oz butter or margarine
1 teaspoon ground ginger	2 tablespoons golden syrup, warmed

Set oven to 350° F or Mark 4. Grease baking sheets. Mix the baking powder, bicarbonate of soda, the spices and lemon peel together in a bowl, sieve in the flour and add the sugar. Mix thoroughly. Rub in the butter or margarine until the mixture resembles breadcrumbs. Add the warmed syrup, using the fingers to combine to a smooth paste, then roll the final mix, with floured hands, into small balls, each about the size of a walnut. Place the balls on the baking sheet, leaving plenty of room between each one. Cook for about 15 minutes then reduce temperature to 325°F or Mark 3 and finish cooking for 5 to 10 minutes so that the biscuits sink and crack into their familiar form. Transfer to a wire rack to cool.

METRIC CONVERSIONS

The weights, measures and oven temperatures used in the preceding recipes can be easily converted to their metric equivalents. The conversions listed below are only approximate, having been rounded up or down as may be appropriate.

Weights

Avoirdupois	Metric
1 oz.	just under 30 grams
4 oz. (¼ lb.)	app. 115 grams
8 oz. (½ lb.)	app. 230 grams
1 lb.	454 grams

Liquid Measures

Imperial	Metric
1 tablespoon (liquid only)	20 millilitres
1 fl. oz.	app. 30 millilitres
1 gill (¼ pt.)	app. 145 millilitres
½ pt.	app. 285 millilitres
1 pt.	app. 570 millilitres
1 qt.	app. 1.140 litres

Oven Temperatures

	°Fahrenheit	Gas Mark	°Celsius
Slow	300	2	150
	325	3	170
Moderate	350	4	180
	375	5	190
	400	6	200
Hot	425	7	220
	450	8	230
	475	9	240

Flour as specified in these recipes refers to plain flour unless otherwise described.